This book belongs to

Summary

Picture of
My Cat

My Pet Profile

Name	
Birthday	
Breed	
Gender	
Coat Color	
Eye Color	
Special Marking	
Weight	
Medical Conditions	
Allergies	
Id Chip #	
Favorite Toys	
Spayed / Neutered	

Vet Details

Vet Name	
Address	
Email	
Phone	

Clinic Details

Hospital Name	
Address	
Email	
Phone	

Vet Visit Log

Date :   Age :

Kind of Visit :   Routine ☐   Emergency ☐

Vet Details	
Reason for visit	
Shots	
Medication	
Other Treatment	
Comments	

Date :   Age :

Kind of Visit :   Routine ☐   Emergency ☐

Vet Details	
Reason for visit	
Shots	
Medication	
Other Treatment	
Comments	

Vet Visit Log

Date :   Age :

Kind of Visit :   Routine ☐   Emergency ☐

Vet Details	
Reason for visit	
Shots	
Medication	
Other Treatment	
Comments	

Date :   Age :

Kind of Visit :   Routine ☐   Emergency ☐

Vet Details	
Reason for visit	
Shots	
Medication	
Other Treatment	
Comments	

Vet Visit Log

Date :   Age :

Kind of Visit :   Routine ☐   Emergency ☐

Vet Details	
Reason for visit	
Shots	
Medication	
Other Treatment	
Comments	

Date :   Age :

Kind of Visit :   Routine ☐   Emergency ☐

Vet Details	
Reason for visit	
Shots	
Medication	
Other Treatment	
Comments	

Vet Visit Log

Date :   Age :

Kind of Visit :   Routine ☐   Emergency ☐

Vet Details	
Reason for visit	
Shots	
Medication	
Other Treatment	
Comments	

....

Date :   Age :

Kind of Visit :   Routine ☐   Emergency ☐

Vet Details	
Reason for visit	
Shots	
Medication	
Other Treatment	
Comments	

Vet Visit Log

Date :   Age :

Kind of Visit :   Routine ☐   Emergency ☐

Vet Details	
Reason for visit	
Shots	
Medication	
Other Treatment	
Comments	

- -

Date :   Age :

Kind of Visit :   Routine ☐   Emergency ☐

Vet Details	
Reason for visit	
Shots	
Medication	
Other Treatment	
Comments	

Vet Visit Log

Date :   Age :

Kind of Visit :   Routine ☐   Emergency ☐

Vet Details	
Reason for visit	
Shots	
Medication	
Other Treatment	
Comments	

Date :   Age :

Kind of Visit :   Routine ☐   Emergency ☐

Vet Details	
Reason for visit	
Shots	
Medication	
Other Treatment	
Comments	

Vet Visit Log

Date :   Age :

Kind of Visit :   Routine ☐   Emergency ☐

Vet Details	
Reason for visit	
Shots	
Medication	
Other Treatment	
Comments	

- -

Date :   Age :

Kind of Visit :   Routine ☐   Emergency ☐

Vet Details	
Reason for visit	
Shots	
Medication	
Other Treatment	
Comments	

Vet Visit Log

Date :   Age :

Kind of Visit :   Routine ☐   Emergency ☐

Vet Details	
Reason for visit	
Shots	
Medication	
Other Treatment	
Comments	

Date :   Age :

Kind of Visit :   Routine ☐   Emergency ☐

Vet Details	
Reason for visit	
Shots	
Medication	
Other Treatment	
Comments	

Vet Visit Log

Date :   Age :

Kind of Visit :   Routine ☐   Emergency ☐

Vet Details	
Reason for visit	
Shots	
Medication	
Other Treatment	
Comments	

Date :   Age :

Kind of Visit :   Routine ☐   Emergency ☐

Vet Details	
Reason for visit	
Shots	
Medication	
Other Treatment	
Comments	

Vet Visit Log

Date :   Age :

Kind of Visit :   Routine ☐   Emergency ☐

Vet Details

Reason for visit

Shots

Medication

Other Treatment

Comments

....

Date :   Age :

Kind of Visit :   Routine ☐   Emergency ☐

Vet Details

Reason for visit

Shots

Medication

Other Treatment

Comments

Vet Visit Log

Date :   Age :

Kind of Visit :   Routine ☐   Emergency ☐

Vet Details	
Reason for visit	
Shots	
Medication	
Other Treatment	
Comments	

- -

Date :   Age :

Kind of Visit :   Routine ☐   Emergency ☐

Vet Details	
Reason for visit	
Shots	
Medication	
Other Treatment	
Comments	

Vet Visit Log

Date :   Age :

Kind of Visit :   Routine ☐   Emergency ☐

Vet Details	
Reason for visit	
Shots	
Medication	
Other Treatment	
Comments	

Date :   Age :

Kind of Visit :   Routine ☐   Emergency ☐

Vet Details	
Reason for visit	
Shots	
Medication	
Other Treatment	
Comments	

Vet Visit Log

Date :   Age :

Kind of Visit :   Routine ☐   Emergency ☐

Vet Details	
Reason for visit	
Shots	
Medication	
Other Treatment	
Comments	

Date :   Age :

Kind of Visit :   Routine ☐   Emergency ☐

Vet Details	
Reason for visit	
Shots	
Medication	
Other Treatment	
Comments	

Vet Visit Log

Date :   Age :

Kind of Visit :   Routine ☐   Emergency ☐

Vet Details	
Reason for visit	
Shots	
Medication	
Other Treatment	
Comments	

Date :   Age :

Kind of Visit :   Routine ☐   Emergency ☐

Vet Details	
Reason for visit	
Shots	
Medication	
Other Treatment	
Comments	

Vet Visit Log

Date :   Age :

Kind of Visit :   Routine ☐   Emergency ☐

Vet Details	
Reason for visit	
Shots	
Medication	
Other Treatment	
Comments	

Date :   Age :

Kind of Visit :   Routine ☐   Emergency ☐

Vet Details	
Reason for visit	
Shots	
Medication	
Other Treatment	
Comments	

Vet Visit Log

Date :   Age :

Kind of Visit :   Routine ☐   Emergency ☐

Vet Details	
Reason for visit	
Shots	
Medication	
Other Treatment	
Comments	

Date :   Age :

Kind of Visit :   Routine ☐   Emergency ☐

Vet Details	
Reason for visit	
Shots	
Medication	
Other Treatment	
Comments	

Vet Visit Log

Date :   Age :

Kind of Visit :   Routine ☐   Emergency ☐

Vet Details	
Reason for visit	
Shots	
Medication	
Other Treatment	
Comments	

Date :   Age :

Kind of Visit :   Routine ☐   Emergency ☐

Vet Details	
Reason for visit	
Shots	
Medication	
Other Treatment	
Comments	

Vet Visit Log

Date :   Age :

Kind of Visit :   Routine ☐   Emergency ☐

Vet Details	
Reason for visit	
Shots	
Medication	
Other Treatment	
Comments	

....

Date :   Age :

Kind of Visit :   Routine ☐   Emergency ☐

Vet Details	
Reason for visit	
Shots	
Medication	
Other Treatment	
Comments	

Vet Visit Log

Date :   Age :

Kind of Visit :   Routine ☐   Emergency ☐

Vet Details	
Reason for visit	
Shots	
Medication	
Other Treatment	
Comments	

Date :   Age :

Kind of Visit :   Routine ☐   Emergency ☐

Vet Details	
Reason for visit	
Shots	
Medication	
Other Treatment	
Comments	

Vet Visit Log

Date :   Age :

Kind of Visit :   Routine ☐   Emergency ☐

Vet Details	
Reason for visit	
Shots	
Medication	
Other Treatment	
Comments	

Date :   Age :

Kind of Visit :   Routine ☐   Emergency ☐

Vet Details	
Reason for visit	
Shots	
Medication	
Other Treatment	
Comments	

Vet Visit Log

Date :   Age :

Kind of Visit :   Routine ☐   Emergency ☐

Vet Details	
Reason for visit	
Shots	
Medication	
Other Treatment	
Comments	

Date :   Age :

Kind of Visit :   Routine ☐   Emergency ☐

Vet Details	
Reason for visit	
Shots	
Medication	
Other Treatment	
Comments	

Vet Visit Log

Date :   Age :

Kind of Visit :   Routine ☐   Emergency ☐

Vet Details	
Reason for visit	
Shots	
Medication	
Other Treatment	
Comments	

- -

Date :   Age :

Kind of Visit :   Routine ☐   Emergency ☐

Vet Details	
Reason for visit	
Shots	
Medication	
Other Treatment	
Comments	

Vet Visit Log

Date :   Age :

Kind of Visit :   Routine ☐   Emergency ☐

Vet Details	
Reason for visit	
Shots	
Medication	
Other Treatment	
Comments	

....

Date :   Age :

Kind of Visit :   Routine ☐   Emergency ☐

Vet Details	
Reason for visit	
Shots	
Medication	
Other Treatment	
Comments	

Vet Visit Log

Date :   Age :

Kind of Visit :   Routine ☐   Emergency ☐

Vet Details	
Reason for visit	
Shots	
Medication	
Other Treatment	
Comments	

Date :   Age :

Kind of Visit :   Routine ☐   Emergency ☐

Vet Details	
Reason for visit	
Shots	
Medication	
Other Treatment	
Comments	

Vet Visit Log

Date :   Age :

Kind of Visit :   Routine ☐   Emergency ☐

Vet Details	
Reason for visit	
Shots	
Medication	
Other Treatment	
Comments	

Date :   Age :

Kind of Visit :   Routine ☐   Emergency ☐

Vet Details	
Reason for visit	
Shots	
Medication	
Other Treatment	
Comments	

Vet Visit Log

Date :   Age :

Kind of Visit :   Routine ☐   Emergency ☐

Vet Details	
Reason for visit	
Shots	
Medication	
Other Treatment	
Comments	

Date :   Age :

Kind of Visit :   Routine ☐   Emergency ☐

Vet Details	
Reason for visit	
Shots	
Medication	
Other Treatment	
Comments	

Vet Visit Log

Date :   Age :

Kind of Visit :   Routine ☐   Emergency ☐

Vet Details	
Reason for visit	
Shots	
Medication	
Other Treatment	
Comments	

Date :   Age :

Kind of Visit :   Routine ☐   Emergency ☐

Vet Details	
Reason for visit	
Shots	
Medication	
Other Treatment	
Comments	

Vet Visit Log

Date :   Age :

Kind of Visit :   Routine ☐   Emergency ☐

Vet Details	
Reason for visit	
Shots	
Medication	
Other Treatment	
Comments	

Date :   Age :

Kind of Visit :   Routine ☐   Emergency ☐

Vet Details	
Reason for visit	
Shots	
Medication	
Other Treatment	
Comments	

Vet Visit Log

Date :   Age :

Kind of Visit :   Routine ☐   Emergency ☐

Vet Details	
Reason for visit	
Shots	
Medication	
Other Treatment	
Comments	

· ·

Date :   Age :

Kind of Visit :   Routine ☐   Emergency ☐

Vet Details	
Reason for visit	
Shots	
Medication	
Other Treatment	
Comments	

Vet Visit Log

Date :   Age :

Kind of Visit :   Routine ☐   Emergency ☐

Vet Details	
Reason for visit	
Shots	
Medication	
Other Treatment	
Comments	

Date :   Age :

Kind of Visit :   Routine ☐   Emergency ☐

Vet Details	
Reason for visit	
Shots	
Medication	
Other Treatment	
Comments	

Vet Visit Log

Date :   Age :

Kind of Visit :   Routine ☐   Emergency ☐

Vet Details	
Reason for visit	
Shots	
Medication	
Other Treatment	
Comments	

Date :   Age :

Kind of Visit :   Routine ☐   Emergency ☐

Vet Details	
Reason for visit	
Shots	
Medication	
Other Treatment	
Comments	

Vet Visit Log

Date :   Age :

Kind of Visit :   Routine ☐   Emergency ☐

Vet Details	
Reason for visit	
Shots	
Medication	
Other Treatment	
Comments	

Date :   Age :

Kind of Visit :   Routine ☐   Emergency ☐

Vet Details	
Reason for visit	
Shots	
Medication	
Other Treatment	
Comments	

Vet Visit Log

Date :   Age :

Kind of Visit :   Routine ☐   Emergency ☐

Vet Details	
Reason for visit	
Shots	
Medication	
Other Treatment	
Comments	

Date :   Age :

Kind of Visit :   Routine ☐   Emergency ☐

Vet Details	
Reason for visit	
Shots	
Medication	
Other Treatment	
Comments	

Vet Visit Log

Date :   Age :

Kind of Visit :   Routine   ☐   Emergency   ☐

Vet Details

Reason for visit

Shots

Medication

Other Treatment

Comments

Date :   Age :

Kind of Visit :   Routine   ☐   Emergency   ☐

Vet Details

Reason for visit

Shots

Medication

Other Treatment

Comments

Vet Visit Log

Date :   Age :

Kind of Visit :   Routine ☐   Emergency ☐

Vet Details	
Reason for visit	
Shots	
Medication	
Other Treatment	
Comments	

- -

Date :   Age :

Kind of Visit :   Routine ☐   Emergency ☐

Vet Details	
Reason for visit	
Shots	
Medication	
Other Treatment	
Comments	

Vet Visit Log

Date : Age :

Kind of Visit : Routine ☐ Emergency ☐

Vet Details	
Reason for visit	
Shots	
Medication	
Other Treatment	
Comments	

Date : Age :

Kind of Visit : Routine ☐ Emergency ☐

Vet Details	
Reason for visit	
Shots	
Medication	
Other Treatment	
Comments	

Vet Visit Log

Date :   Age :

Kind of Visit :   Routine ☐   Emergency ☐

Vet Details	
Reason for visit	
Shots	
Medication	
Other Treatment	
Comments	

Date :   Age :

Kind of Visit :   Routine ☐   Emergency ☐

Vet Details	
Reason for visit	
Shots	
Medication	
Other Treatment	
Comments	

Vet Visit Log

Date :   Age :

Kind of Visit :   Routine ☐   Emergency ☐

Vet Details	
Reason for visit	
Shots	
Medication	
Other Treatment	
Comments	

Date :   Age :

Kind of Visit :   Routine ☐   Emergency ☐

Vet Details	
Reason for visit	
Shots	
Medication	
Other Treatment	
Comments	

Vet Visit Log

Date :   Age :

Kind of Visit :   Routine ☐   Emergency ☐

Vet Details	
Reason for visit	
Shots	
Medication	
Other Treatment	
Comments	

Date :   Age :

Kind of Visit :   Routine ☐   Emergency ☐

Vet Details	
Reason for visit	
Shots	
Medication	
Other Treatment	
Comments	

Vet Visit Log

Date :   Age :

Kind of Visit :   Routine ☐   Emergency ☐

Vet Details	
Reason for visit	
Shots	
Medication	
Other Treatment	
Comments	

- -

Date :   Age :

Kind of Visit :   Routine ☐   Emergency ☐

Vet Details	
Reason for visit	
Shots	
Medication	
Other Treatment	
Comments	

Vet Visit Log

Date :   Age :

Kind of Visit :   Routine ☐   Emergency ☐

Vet Details	
Reason for visit	
Shots	
Medication	
Other Treatment	
Comments	

- -

Date :   Age :

Kind of Visit :   Routine ☐   Emergency ☐

Vet Details	
Reason for visit	
Shots	
Medication	
Other Treatment	
Comments	

Vet Visit Log

Date :   Age :

Kind of Visit :   Routine ☐   Emergency ☐

Vet Details	
Reason for visit	
Shots	
Medication	
Other Treatment	
Comments	

Date :   Age :

Kind of Visit :   Routine ☐   Emergency ☐

Vet Details	
Reason for visit	
Shots	
Medication	
Other Treatment	
Comments	

Vet Visit Log

Date :   Age :

Kind of Visit :   Routine ☐   Emergency ☐

Vet Details	
Reason for visit	
Shots	
Medication	
Other Treatment	
Comments	

....

Date :   Age :

Kind of Visit :   Routine ☐   Emergency ☐

Vet Details	
Reason for visit	
Shots	
Medication	
Other Treatment	
Comments	

Vet Visit Log

Date :   Age :

Kind of Visit :   Routine ☐   Emergency ☐

Vet Details	
Reason for visit	
Shots	
Medication	
Other Treatment	
Comments	

Date :   Age :

Kind of Visit :   Routine ☐   Emergency ☐

Vet Details	
Reason for visit	
Shots	
Medication	
Other Treatment	
Comments	

Vet Visit Log

Date :   Age :

Kind of Visit :   Routine ☐   Emergency ☐

Vet Details	
Reason for visit	
Shots	
Medication	
Other Treatment	
Comments	

Date :   Age :

Kind of Visit :   Routine ☐   Emergency ☐

Vet Details	
Reason for visit	
Shots	
Medication	
Other Treatment	
Comments	

Vet Visit Log

Date :   Age :

Kind of Visit :   Routine ☐   Emergency ☐

Vet Details	
Reason for visit	
Shots	
Medication	
Other Treatment	
Comments	

. . . .

Date :   Age :

Kind of Visit :   Routine ☐   Emergency ☐

Vet Details	
Reason for visit	
Shots	
Medication	
Other Treatment	
Comments	

Vet Visit Log

Date :   Age :

Kind of Visit :   Routine ☐   Emergency ☐

Vet Details	
Reason for visit	
Shots	
Medication	
Other Treatment	
Comments	

Date :   Age :

Kind of Visit :   Routine ☐   Emergency ☐

Vet Details	
Reason for visit	
Shots	
Medication	
Other Treatment	
Comments	

Vet Visit Log

Date :   Age :

Kind of Visit :   Routine ☐   Emergency ☐

Vet Details	
Reason for visit	
Shots	
Medication	
Other Treatment	
Comments	

Date :   Age :

Kind of Visit :   Routine ☐   Emergency ☐

Vet Details	
Reason for visit	
Shots	
Medication	
Other Treatment	
Comments	

Vet Visit Log

Date :   Age :

Kind of Visit :   Routine ☐   Emergency ☐

Vet Details	
Reason for visit	
Shots	
Medication	
Other Treatment	
Comments	

- -

Date :   Age :

Kind of Visit :   Routine ☐   Emergency ☐

Vet Details	
Reason for visit	
Shots	
Medication	
Other Treatment	
Comments	

Vet Visit Log

Date :   Age :

Kind of Visit :   Routine ☐   Emergency ☐

Vet Details	
Reason for visit	
Shots	
Medication	
Other Treatment	
Comments	

Date :   Age :

Kind of Visit :   Routine ☐   Emergency ☐

Vet Details	
Reason for visit	
Shots	
Medication	
Other Treatment	
Comments	

Vet Visit Log

Date :   Age :

Kind of Visit :   Routine ☐   Emergency ☐

Vet Details	
Reason for visit	
Shots	
Medication	
Other Treatment	
Comments	

- -

Date :   Age :

Kind of Visit :   Routine ☐   Emergency ☐

Vet Details	
Reason for visit	
Shots	
Medication	
Other Treatment	
Comments	

Vet Visit Log

Date :   Age :

Kind of Visit :   Routine ☐   Emergency ☐

Vet Details

Reason for visit

Shots

Medication

Other Treatment

Comments

Date :   Age :

Kind of Visit :   Routine ☐   Emergency ☐

Vet Details

Reason for visit

Shots

Medication

Other Treatment

Comments

Vet Visit Log

Date :   Age :

Kind of Visit :   Routine ☐   Emergency ☐

Vet Details	
Reason for visit	
Shots	
Medication	
Other Treatment	
Comments	

. . . .

Date :   Age :

Kind of Visit :   Routine ☐   Emergency ☐

Vet Details	
Reason for visit	
Shots	
Medication	
Other Treatment	
Comments	

Vet Visit Log

Date :   Age :

Kind of Visit :   Routine ☐   Emergency ☐

Vet Details	
Reason for visit	
Shots	
Medication	
Other Treatment	
Comments	

Date :   Age :

Kind of Visit :   Routine ☐   Emergency ☐

Vet Details	
Reason for visit	
Shots	
Medication	
Other Treatment	
Comments	

Vet Visit Log

Date :   Age :

Kind of Visit :   Routine ☐   Emergency ☐

Vet Details	
Reason for visit	
Shots	
Medication	
Other Treatment	
Comments	

· ·

Date :   Age :

Kind of Visit :   Routine ☐   Emergency ☐

Vet Details	
Reason for visit	
Shots	
Medication	
Other Treatment	
Comments	

Vet Visit Log

Date :   Age :

Kind of Visit :   Routine ☐   Emergency ☐

Vet Details	
Reason for visit	
Shots	
Medication	
Other Treatment	
Comments	

Date :   Age :

Kind of Visit :   Routine ☐   Emergency ☐

Vet Details	
Reason for visit	
Shots	
Medication	
Other Treatment	
Comments	

Vet Visit Log

Date :   Age :

Kind of Visit :   Routine ☐   Emergency ☐

Vet Details	
Reason for visit	
Shots	
Medication	
Other Treatment	
Comments	

Date :   Age :

Kind of Visit :   Routine ☐   Emergency ☐

Vet Details	
Reason for visit	
Shots	
Medication	
Other Treatment	
Comments	

Vet Visit Log

Date :   Age :

Kind of Visit :   Routine ☐   Emergency ☐

Vet Details

Reason for visit

Shots

Medication

Other Treatment

Comments

Date :   Age :

Kind of Visit :   Routine ☐   Emergency ☐

Vet Details

Reason for visit

Shots

Medication

Other Treatment

Comments

Vet Visit Log

Date :   Age :

Kind of Visit :   Routine ☐   Emergency ☐

Vet Details	
Reason for visit	
Shots	
Medication	
Other Treatment	
Comments	

- -

Date :   Age :

Kind of Visit :   Routine ☐   Emergency ☐

Vet Details	
Reason for visit	
Shots	
Medication	
Other Treatment	
Comments	

Vet Visit Log

Date :   Age :

Kind of Visit :   Routine ☐   Emergency ☐

Vet Details	
Reason for visit	
Shots	
Medication	
Other Treatment	
Comments	

- -

Date :   Age :

Kind of Visit :   Routine ☐   Emergency ☐

Vet Details	
Reason for visit	
Shots	
Medication	
Other Treatment	
Comments	

Vet Visit Log

Date :   Age :

Kind of Visit :   Routine ☐   Emergency ☐

Vet Details	
Reason for visit	
Shots	
Medication	
Other Treatment	
Comments	

....

Date :   Age :

Kind of Visit :   Routine ☐   Emergency ☐

Vet Details	
Reason for visit	
Shots	
Medication	
Other Treatment	
Comments	

Vet Visit Log

Date :   Age :

Kind of Visit :   Routine ☐   Emergency ☐

Vet Details	
Reason for visit	
Shots	
Medication	
Other Treatment	
Comments	

Date :   Age :

Kind of Visit :   Routine ☐   Emergency ☐

Vet Details	
Reason for visit	
Shots	
Medication	
Other Treatment	
Comments	

Vet Visit Log

Date :   Age :

Kind of Visit :   Routine ☐   Emergency ☐

Vet Details	
Reason for visit	
Shots	
Medication	
Other Treatment	
Comments	

- -

Date :   Age :

Kind of Visit :   Routine ☐   Emergency ☐

Vet Details	
Reason for visit	
Shots	
Medication	
Other Treatment	
Comments	

Vet Visit Log

Date :   Age :

Kind of Visit :   Routine ☐   Emergency ☐

Vet Details

Reason for visit

Shots

Medication

Other Treatment

Comments

Date :   Age :

Kind of Visit :   Routine ☐   Emergency ☐

Vet Details

Reason for visit

Shots

Medication

Other Treatment

Comments

Vet Visit Log

Date :   Age :

Kind of Visit :   Routine ☐   Emergency ☐

Vet Details	
Reason for visit	
Shots	
Medication	
Other Treatment	
Comments	

Date :   Age :

Kind of Visit :   Routine ☐   Emergency ☐

Vet Details	
Reason for visit	
Shots	
Medication	
Other Treatment	
Comments	

Vet Visit Log

Date :   Age :

Kind of Visit :   Routine ☐   Emergency ☐

Vet Details	
Reason for visit	
Shots	
Medication	
Other Treatment	
Comments	

- -

Date :   Age :

Kind of Visit :   Routine ☐   Emergency ☐

Vet Details	
Reason for visit	
Shots	
Medication	
Other Treatment	
Comments	

Vet Visit Log

Date :   Age :

Kind of Visit :   Routine ☐   Emergency ☐

Vet Details	
Reason for visit	
Shots	
Medication	
Other Treatment	
Comments	

- -

Date :   Age :

Kind of Visit :   Routine ☐   Emergency ☐

Vet Details	
Reason for visit	
Shots	
Medication	
Other Treatment	
Comments	

Vet Visit Log

Date :   Age :

Kind of Visit :   Routine ☐   Emergency ☐

Vet Details	
Reason for visit	
Shots	
Medication	
Other Treatment	
Comments	

Date :   Age :

Kind of Visit :   Routine ☐   Emergency ☐

Vet Details	
Reason for visit	
Shots	
Medication	
Other Treatment	
Comments	

Vet Visit Log

Date :   Age :

Kind of Visit :   Routine ☐   Emergency ☐

Vet Details	
Reason for visit	
Shots	
Medication	
Other Treatment	
Comments	

Date :   Age :

Kind of Visit :   Routine ☐   Emergency ☐

Vet Details	
Reason for visit	
Shots	
Medication	
Other Treatment	
Comments	

Vet Visit Log

Date :   Age :

Kind of Visit :   Routine ☐   Emergency ☐

Vet Details

Reason for visit

Shots

Medication

Other Treatment

Comments

Date :   Age :

Kind of Visit :   Routine ☐   Emergency ☐

Vet Details

Reason for visit

Shots

Medication

Other Treatment

Comments

Vet Visit Log

Date :   Age :

Kind of Visit :   Routine ☐   Emergency ☐

Vet Details	
Reason for visit	
Shots	
Medication	
Other Treatment	
Comments	

....

Date :   Age :

Kind of Visit :   Routine ☐   Emergency ☐

Vet Details	
Reason for visit	
Shots	
Medication	
Other Treatment	
Comments	

Vet Visit Log

Date :   Age :

Kind of Visit :   Routine ☐   Emergency ☐

Vet Details	

Reason for visit	
Shots	
Medication	
Other Treatment	
Comments	

- -

Date :   Age :

Kind of Visit :   Routine ☐   Emergency ☐

Vet Details	

Reason for visit	
Shots	
Medication	
Other Treatment	
Comments	

Vet Visit Log

Date :   Age :

Kind of Visit :   Routine ☐   Emergency ☐

Vet Details	
Reason for visit	
Shots	
Medication	
Other Treatment	
Comments	

Date :   Age :

Kind of Visit :   Routine ☐   Emergency ☐

Vet Details	
Reason for visit	
Shots	
Medication	
Other Treatment	
Comments	

Vet Visit Log

Date :   Age :

Kind of Visit :   Routine ☐   Emergency ☐

Vet Details	
Reason for visit	
Shots	
Medication	
Other Treatment	
Comments	

Date :   Age :

Kind of Visit :   Routine ☐   Emergency ☐

Vet Details	
Reason for visit	
Shots	
Medication	
Other Treatment	
Comments	

Vet Visit Log

Date :   Age :

Kind of Visit :   Routine ☐   Emergency ☐

Vet Details	
Reason for visit	
Shots	
Medication	
Other Treatment	
Comments	

Date :   Age :

Kind of Visit :   Routine ☐   Emergency ☐

Vet Details	
Reason for visit	
Shots	
Medication	
Other Treatment	
Comments	

Vet Visit Log

Date :   Age :

Kind of Visit :   Routine ☐   Emergency ☐

Vet Details

Reason for visit

Shots

Medication

Other Treatment

Comments

- -

Date :   Age :

Kind of Visit :   Routine ☐   Emergency ☐

Vet Details

Reason for visit

Shots

Medication

Other Treatment

Comments

Vet Visit Log

Date :   Age :

Kind of Visit :   Routine ☐   Emergency ☐

Vet Details	
Reason for visit	
Shots	
Medication	
Other Treatment	
Comments	

Date :   Age :

Kind of Visit :   Routine ☐   Emergency ☐

Vet Details	
Reason for visit	
Shots	
Medication	
Other Treatment	
Comments	

Vet Visit Log

Date :   Age :

Kind of Visit :   Routine ☐   Emergency ☐

Vet Details	
Reason for visit	
Shots	
Medication	
Other Treatment	
Comments	

. . . .

Date :   Age :

Kind of Visit :   Routine ☐   Emergency ☐

Vet Details	
Reason for visit	
Shots	
Medication	
Other Treatment	
Comments	

Vet Visit Log

Date :   Age :

Kind of Visit :   Routine ☐   Emergency ☐

Vet Details	
Reason for visit	
Shots	
Medication	
Other Treatment	
Comments	

Date :   Age :

Kind of Visit :   Routine ☐   Emergency ☐

Vet Details	
Reason for visit	
Shots	
Medication	
Other Treatment	
Comments	

Vet Visit Log

Date :   Age :

Kind of Visit :   Routine ☐   Emergency ☐

Vet Details	
Reason for visit	
Shots	
Medication	
Other Treatment	
Comments	

Date :   Age :

Kind of Visit :   Routine ☐   Emergency ☐

Vet Details	
Reason for visit	
Shots	
Medication	
Other Treatment	
Comments	

Vet Visit Log

Date :   Age :

Kind of Visit :   Routine ☐   Emergency ☐

Vet Details	
Reason for visit	
Shots	
Medication	
Other Treatment	
Comments	

- -

Date :   Age :

Kind of Visit :   Routine ☐   Emergency ☐

Vet Details	
Reason for visit	
Shots	
Medication	
Other Treatment	
Comments	

Vet Visit Log

Date :   Age :

Kind of Visit :   Routine ☐   Emergency ☐

Vet Details	
Reason for visit	
Shots	
Medication	
Other Treatment	
Comments	

Date :   Age :

Kind of Visit :   Routine ☐   Emergency ☐

Vet Details	
Reason for visit	
Shots	
Medication	
Other Treatment	
Comments	

Vet Visit Log

Date :   Age :

Kind of Visit :   Routine ☐   Emergency ☐

Vet Details	
Reason for visit	
Shots	
Medication	
Other Treatment	
Comments	

Date :   Age :

Kind of Visit :   Routine ☐   Emergency ☐

Vet Details	
Reason for visit	
Shots	
Medication	
Other Treatment	
Comments	

Vet Visit Log

Date :   Age :

Kind of Visit :   Routine ☐   Emergency ☐

Vet Details

Reason for visit

Shots

Medication

Other Treatment

Comments

. . . .

Date :   Age :

Kind of Visit :   Routine ☐   Emergency ☐

Vet Details

Reason for visit

Shots

Medication

Other Treatment

Comments

Vet Visit Log

Date :   Age :

Kind of Visit :   Routine ☐   Emergency ☐

Vet Details	
Reason for visit	
Shots	
Medication	
Other Treatment	
Comments	

- -

Date :   Age :

Kind of Visit :   Routine ☐   Emergency ☐

Vet Details	
Reason for visit	
Shots	
Medication	
Other Treatment	
Comments	

Vet Visit Log

Date :   Age :

Kind of Visit :   Routine ☐   Emergency ☐

Vet Details	
Reason for visit	
Shots	
Medication	
Other Treatment	
Comments	

Date :   Age :

Kind of Visit :   Routine ☐   Emergency ☐

Vet Details	
Reason for visit	
Shots	
Medication	
Other Treatment	
Comments	

Vet Visit Log

Date :   Age :

Kind of Visit :   Routine ☐   Emergency ☐

Vet Details	
Reason for visit	
Shots	
Medication	
Other Treatment	
Comments	

Date :   Age :

Kind of Visit :   Routine ☐   Emergency ☐

Vet Details	
Reason for visit	
Shots	
Medication	
Other Treatment	
Comments	

Vet Visit Log

Date :   Age :

Kind of Visit :   Routine ☐   Emergency ☐

Vet Details

Reason for visit

Shots

Medication

Other Treatment

Comments

Date :   Age :

Kind of Visit :   Routine ☐   Emergency ☐

Vet Details

Reason for visit

Shots

Medication

Other Treatment

Comments

Vaccination Log

Date	Vaccination	Age	Notes

Vaccination Log

Date	Vaccination	Age	Notes

Notes

Notes

Notes

Notes

Made in the USA
Coppell, TX
10 February 2023